the *voice*
of
gratitude

celebrating *the* gift *of* friendship

MICHELLE MARIE SORRO

 Seven Publishing · Santa Monica, California

SEVEN PUBLISHING
P.O. Box 1123
Santa Monica, CA 90404-1123
seven@sevenpublishing.com
www.sevenpublishing.com
www.michellesorro.com
(877) 595-6996

the voice of gratitude © 2003 by Michelle Marie Sorro

Seven Publishing First Edition 2003
Manufactured in the United States of America

ISBN 0-9723578-5-8

Book Design by Ron Hobart

Dust Jacket Design by Kathi Dunn of Dunn+Associates
www.dunn-design.com

Printing by Central Plains Book Manufacturing
www.centralplainsbook.com

Dedicated to friendships everywhere.

Introduction

A few years ago I began a gratitude journal and watched my life transform. As I expressed gratitude for the significant people and otherwise ordinary moments in my life, I literally felt my heart open to a profound sense of love and appreciation.

Everyone wants to feel significant. And expressing genuine gratitude for one another fulfills this universal need. It really is that simple. With this expanded gratitude awareness, I awakened to a sense of destiny in myself and felt compelled to share my voice of gratitude with the world.

This book was inspired by the beautiful relationships in my life and many others I have had the honor to observe. Though your declarations may be different, I do hope mine gives voice to the grateful heart within you. I thank you for being The Voice of Gratitude as you share these heartfelt statements with the people you love.

Love,
Michelle Marie Sorro

Hold a true friendship with both hands.

~NIGERIAN PROVERB

I'm grateful you understand where I've been

. . . accept who I've become

. . . and encourage me to grow.

I'm grateful you stay aware of my dreams
and if I forget, you are there to remind me.

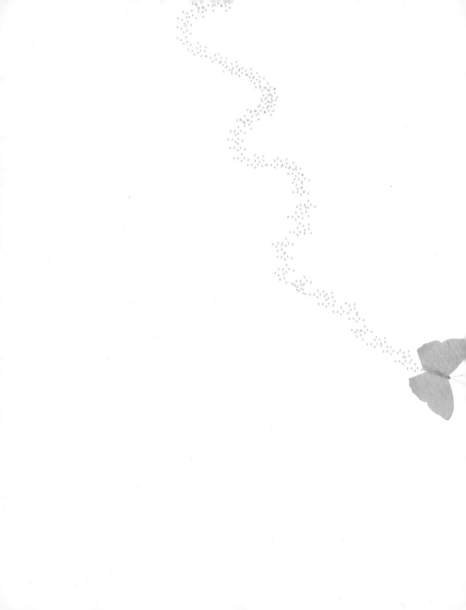

I'm grateful for your gently reminding me
that I always have choices in life.

I'm grateful I can always count on your rowdy enthusiasm of support.

I'm grateful I never have to explain myself to you
... you just "get" me.

I'm grateful for your encouraging my confidence
and not allowing me to play small.

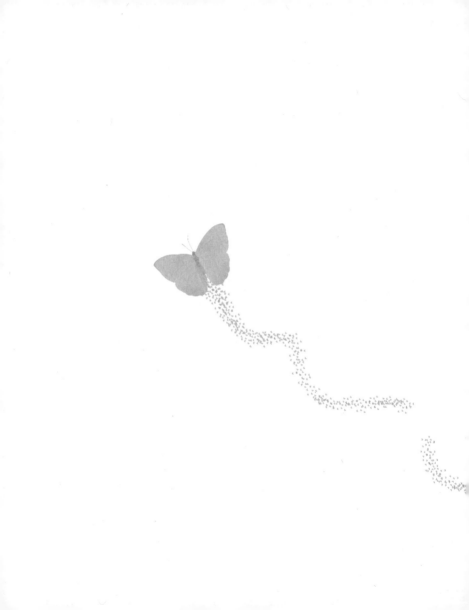

I'm grateful for your accepting my uniqueness without judgment.

I'm grateful for your encouraging my
strengths without competition.

I'm grateful for the finite wisdom
you consistently bring to our friendship.

I'm grateful for how the sincerity
in our friendship shows me
an authentic reflection of myself.

I'm grateful for your sense of adventure
and zany spontaneity.

I'm grateful for your being brave enough
to offer up your unabashed honesty
. . . when no one else will.

I'm grateful we found each other
...what would life be like without you?

I'm grateful for our always interesting conversations about sometimes nothing at all.

I'm grateful you don't shame me
when I say something I wish I could take back.

I'm grateful for your thoughtful,
lighthearted nature.

I'm grateful you remind me to let go
of expectations and to have trust
in the bigger picture.

I'm grateful for your teaching me how
to be a better friend.

I'm grateful for your telling me
how fabulous I look,
just when I need to hear it the most.

I'm grateful I'm bursting with gratefuls for you!

I'm grateful that you listen to how I could improve
my life and if I don't change a thing,
you still respect me.

I'm grateful for your unconditional
and sustained loyalty.

I'm grateful that you never tell me
what I should do, but remind me
what I could do.

I'm grateful you help keep me accountable to myself.

I'm grateful that you help me feel
like the brightest, hippest
and most talented person alive.

I'm grateful for the effervescent vibe
you bring into a room
. . . just by being in it.

I'm grateful for your reminding me
how significant I am
...when I feel lonely inside.

I'm grateful for how we raise the bar in having fun.

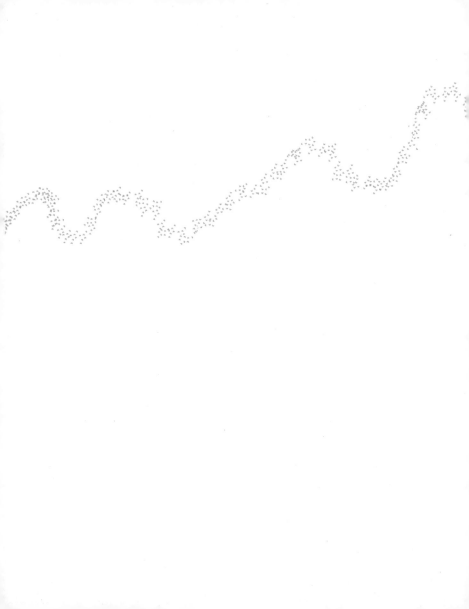

I'm grateful for your validating my point of view
. . . even when you disagree.

I'm grateful you've given me meaning
to the word friend.

I'm grateful for your patient listening
in my times of disappointment.

I'm grateful for the inspirational touchstone
you give me to be the best "me" I can be.

I'm grateful because you love me.

I'm grateful for our laugh-out-loud
kind of days together!

*I'm grateful you trust me to be honest with you...
when it counts the most.*

I'm grateful you know just when to remind me
not to take life too seriously.

I'm grateful that you're strong enough
to catch my occasional attitude
...and wise enough to let it go.

I'm grateful you laugh
at my silly indulgences in life.

I'm grateful you sincerely believe
I deserve the best
and never want me to settle for less.

I'm grateful my heart has expanded in gratitude
because I know you.

I'm grateful because, without your friendship
. . . I wouldn't be the same.

And, if there is ever a moment you forget
how significant you are,

I invite you to open any page of this book
to be reminded of your importance
again and again.

This is the time to acknowledge and celebrate
the blessings in our lives...

Thank you friend, for inspiring me to be

the *Voice*

of

Gratitude.

Acknowledgments

This book was inspired by the many blessings in my life…

My best friend Brooke— I am truly honored by your friendship. Dad— you are my sunshine. Chris, David, Laura, Britney, David Jr., Christopher & Kitty— wa, wa, wu dear family. Keisha— my sister and longest friend, I love you puss. For my 'safety adventure' circle of friends— Michelley, Eric, Daniel, Jan, Lex, Brandi, Kym, Jimela, Darlene & Baby Walsh— I'm grateful for the colors you bring to my life. Author Power and especially Eric— for whose endless support and accountability kept the flow of this book moving with ease and grace. Erick— awr… thank you for opening my world to infinite possibilities. Agape— Rev. Dr. Michael Beckwith— for being my center of truth and well-being. Oprah— thank you for giving me back to myself. Mark Victor Hansen— ah, my mentor and inspirational touchstone. And for my Mama— mmn… there are no words — you are everything and more.

Of course my deepest gratitude is for Life itself. I am thankful to be aware of the blessings in every moment. I am grateful…

Expand your Heart

Be the Voice of Gratitude

♥

Do you feel grateful for a particular time, experience or moment that shifted your awareness to more appreciation and gratitude for your life?

If yes, we would love to hear from you. We encourage you to be a contributor to life, as you and many others share personalized thanksgivings, stories and sentiments for our upcoming books in gratitude.

Please contact us:

www.michellesorro.com